ADVENTURES IN

PARENTING

BOOK 1 The Playdate

Written by
DR. ROB DANIELS &
ADAM HIEBELER

Illustrated by
BONNIE L. MILLARD

Acknowledgments

All projects require the support of others, and this book is certainly no exception. I could not have placed any of these words on the page without the dedication, humor, and skill of my coauthor, Adam. It has been a true pleasure collaborating with such a generous, talented author.

Personally, my life would not be complete without my own partner in parenting and nearly every other adventure in my life, my intelligent, classy, beautiful wife, Amy. Our three children, Taylor, Emma, and Carter, fill my life with joy as I watch them grow up to be independent individuals with their own dreams, strengths, and endearing personalities.

My parents provided me with no shortage of adventures, and I cherish the memories of the ones in the past; and look forward to the ones we will create together in the future. While my father cannot join me in any additional adventures, since he passed away in November 2017, I know that he would be experiencing "nachas" as his baby boy grew up to be a published author.

The hundreds of my former clients who shared their adventures with me and granted me the honor of being their psychologist and confidant taught me at least as much as I could have taught them. Their love and dedication to their children has always been an inspiration to me, as they demonstrated time and again that they would do anything to help their children overcome their challenges and demonstrate their inner strengths.

A final shout out to our incredible illustrator, Bonnie, who took the black letters on a white background and converted them into a vibrant set of images that helped tell our story.

Dr. Rob Daniels

Acknowledgments

"We're moving to Chicago?!" I cried to my parents in the summer of 1986, feeling hung out to dry between 6th and 7th grade. "It's an adventure!" they declared with equal parts pure excitement and, what I now suspect, sheer terror. But of all the choices I've either made—or been coerced to go along with—few compare to this choice my parents made for our family. Because this one led me to the woman I was meant to find. She made me a husband, a father, and a man. And nothing brings me more joy than having such a strong, smart, fun, beautiful, and loving partner by my side to shepherd our gems, Holden and Ruby, through life's ups and downs. Carrie, I dedicate this book and all the volumes to come, to you and the stories we write together every day. I love you forever. And to my parents, I cannot say "Thank you!" enough for having the courage to make that critical choice and for teaching me the value of a great adventure.

Whenever I meet a psychologist, whether at a Pump It Up party, a Little League game, or in the driveway next door, the first question I ask myself is *"Are you reading my mind?"* Rob Daniels is a brilliant mind who has an uncanny knack for cutting through the nonsense and finding the simplest, most human solutions to help children and their parents. It's a rare gift and I'm honored to have been entrusted with bringing his life's work to life. Thank you, Rob, for your down to earth, self-deprecating observations, for inviting me along on this journey, and for not reading my mind (as far as I know).

Adventures have many paths and when those paths cross, good things happen. I'm delighted to have crossed paths with Bonnie Millard several times in my career and this time is no exception. I know our readers will enjoy seeing these stories reflected in her charming illustrations as much as I do.

Adam Hiebeler

Forward

Parents frequently are their own harshest critics. We second-guess ourselves, worry if we've made the right decision, and often simply operate on "auto-pilot" with a hope that things will turn out okay. While there's a range from laissez-faire to helicopter parenting styles, the reality is that there isn't one and only one correct way to parent your child. In fact, there are hundreds of equally viable alternative methods of parenting that each have their strengths and benefits. If you ask 100 psychologists any question about parenting, they will provide at least 100 opinions, but one opinion that they will all share is that the correct answer to every question in psychology is, "It depends." What if I make a mistake? It depends, perhaps you'll learn from that mistake and you might not have learned that lesson had you guessed correctly, instead.

Adventures in Parenting is a fun, fictional narrative that allows you to learn from the experiences of the characters that positive outcomes are possible, even if you make mistakes. The best outcomes occur after a series of good decisions, but the worst outcomes don't usually occur after only one mistake. The worst outcomes come after a series of bad decisions. Another thing on which most psychologists, parents, and grandparents will agree is that mistakes are inevitable, and no one can predict the future. However, if you repeatedly make the same types of mistakes, it becomes easy to predict that the outcomes will be bad. Conversely, if you repeatedly attempt to plan ahead, exercise realistic optimism, and reinforce your child's good decisions, positive outcomes are quite likely.

So, feel free to experiment as you make decisions on behalf of the characters in these books. We've enjoyed heightening the intensity of the outcomes to illustrate the lessons contained in the story. Forgive our hyperbole. There's enough reality infused in these fictional pages, based on our own parenting successes and failures, that you can rest assured that we feel your pain, and we share your joys. The stories are brief. We know that parents of young children don't have time to read several hundreds of pages, regardless of how good the advice contained within them may be. Lock the door to your bathroom, read a short story, chuckle at how ridiculous life with children may be, and then return to "the battlefield" of skinned knees, spilled milk, arguments over everything, and, occasionally, laughter, joy, warmth, kindness and love.

"Mommy, I'm bored," protests Sadie, your infinitely curious and preciously precocious 6-year-old daughter as you finish loading the dishwasher. It's 9AM. Monday. But not just any Monday. Columbus Day. No school for Sadie. And, unfortunately, no rest for the emails piling up in your inbox with a relentless string of BEEPS and CHIRPS coming from your phone—just out of arm's reach on the kitchen counter.

As you wipe away a dot of syrup on your watch, you discover that it's been exactly one hour since you embarked on Sadie's favorite breakfast—French toast with hand-whipped cream, chocolate chips, and fresh strawberries.

"Gimme a sec, Sadie." It's an innocent plea. One you'll make once, twice, a dozen times before the day is over. Maybe more because this day is different. Today you're expecting final client comments on a grant proposal you've been writing for the last 3 months. And, judging by the racket coming from your phone, the comments are trickling in one at a time like some sort of Chinese water torture.

So, you cave. And pick up your phone. And slip into zombie, autopilot mode. Scanning and swiping as your eyes glaze over and your brain travels to a place where perfectly normal people start acting anything but normal under the pressure of a potentially lucrative deadline.

"Mom," Sadie reminds you, "I'm bored! I want a playdate!"

And then it happens. *PING.* A text from Kim, your college roommate who just moved in a few miles away: "Help! Jeff still in Hong Kong. Need adult conversation. Bring Sadie. Girls can play."

If you text Kim back and say, "We'll be right over,"
turn to page 2.

If you ask Sadie what she wants to do,
turn to page 34.

You text Kim back and say, "We'll be right over"

"Grab Holly, honey. You and Elizabeth can play dolls," you announce as you grab your car keys.

Sadie is slow to move. "Are you going to work?" she asks, pointing to the laptop poking out of your purse.

"No. We're going to play," you explain. "It's gonna be fun."

Sadie grabs her favorite yarn doll, Holly, and follows you to the car. It's a short ride to Kim's house, but Sadie seems unusually quiet.

"What's wrong, Sadie?" you ask, stealing glances at your phone as you drive.

"Nothing," Sadie responds.

You put down your phone to read Sadie's body language in the rearview mirror.

"It doesn't seem like nothing," you probe. "What is it? I thought you were bored."

After a few more silent blocks, Sadie finally comes clean. "Elizabeth doesn't like dolls."

If you pull over to have a quick chat about what's on Sadie's mind,
turn to page 3.

If you just keep driving, hoping Sadie will come around,
turn to page 22.

You pull over to have a quick chat about what's on Sadie's mind

"Are we here already?" Sadie asks, none too thrilled.

"No, honey," you explain as you put the car in park and turn around to face her in the backseat. "Why do you think Elizabeth doesn't like dolls?"

"She told me they're dumb," Sadie reveals, "when I saw her at the grocery store."

That's right. You recall running into Kim and Elizabeth a few weeks back at the deli counter. Kim looked exhausted. And Elizabeth was late for soccer.

"Maybe she was just hungry, Sadie," you offer. "Sometimes people get a little crabby when they need a snack."

"Like Dad when he can't find his potato chips?" Sadie giggles.

"Yeah. Just like that," you answer back with a smile. "Maybe there's something else you could play? Like dress-ups? Or bakery? Didn't she get a play kitchen for her birthday?"

Nothing sticks. Sadie just looks lost.

"Can you tell me what you're thinking about?" you ask.

"She's just really bossy," Sadie explains.

"That must make you feel pretty frustrated," you acknowledge.

Sadie nods her head. "Why can't I just play by myself?"

"Because I'd really like to see you guys get along. Her mom is a good friend and it's nice to learn how to be friends. You can never have too many friends, you know."

Sadie warms up a little. She likes the idea of having friends.

"I tell you what," you offer. "I'll watch how the two of you get along, and come up with some suggestions. I might suggest you take turns. First, Elizabeth's idea, then your idea, like that. Or, I might come up with an idea. If you try to be patient, play her game nicely, and agree to the plan we come up with, that would make me so proud of you. And, do you know what I love to do when I am proud of you?"

"What?" Elizabeth asks.

"I like to do nice things for YOU! What is something nice I could do for you after you play nicely with Elizabeth?"

Sadie gets excited. "Could we buy a new dress for Holly? Please!"

You answer happily, "Yes, that is an EXCELLENT idea. Remember, be patient, try her ideas and my ideas, and play nicely. If you do those things, we will go and get a new dress for Holly. Deal?"

Sadie hugs Holly tightly. "Deal," she agrees as you pull back onto the road.

Turn to page 4.   3

"Can I ring the doorbell, Mommy?" Sadie asks as you approach Kim's house. Sadie loves doorbells and you're happy to have her interest.

"Go for it, sweetie," you encourage her.

She proudly lifts her finger and pushes the button. Ding-dong! You both wait patiently, but there's no signs of life coming from inside. Sadie giggles as she pushes the button again. Twice in rapid succession.

"Sadie! Don't be rude," you admonish. "We're in no rush."

After a few more seconds of uncomfortable silence, you decide to knock. And just as you raise your knuckles to the door, it opens.

"Sorry, you guys! I was having a little chat with Elizabeth," Kim explains.

"Mommy, I don't want to clean my room!" you hear Elizabeth complain from somewhere inside the house.

"Elizabeth, clean your room right now." Kim yells.

"No!" Elizabeth replies rudely.

"I'll give you a cupcake, okay?" Kim responds.

"For breakfast?!" Sadie wonders aloud, adding an uneasy layer of chagrin.

As you make your way to the kitchen, you notice the house is a mess. Shoes in the hallway. A jump rope in the living room. Food wrappers in the bathroom.

"So, when does Jeff come back?" you probe as you arrive in the kitchen, stacked with dirty dishes.

"Elizabeth?" Kim deflects. "Sadie's here!"

No reply. Sadie looks uneasy. Can you blame her?

Then, finally, from the basement stairs you hear, "I'm down here."

If you let Sadie play with Elizabeth unsupervised in the basement,
turn to page 23.

If you try to urge Elizabeth to come play upstairs,
turn to page 28.

You leave the girls to work it out on their own

"He barely calls. And when he does, the time zones are completely flipped. It's taking a toll on Elizabeth, too," Kim confides. "Her attitude has been just awful while he's away. Talking back. Refusing to go to bed. It's been a nightmare."

You take Kim's frustrations to heart, wanting to help her while your phone continues to BUZZ in your pocket. "When does he come back?" you inquire.

"Sunday," Kim explains. "But Elizabeth has two birthday parties and a soccer game. He's going to be a zombie."

Knock! Knock! You turn to find Sadie clawing at the patio door. She doesn't look happy. But Kim is on the brink of tears. She seems to really need you to listen right now.

If you interrupt Kim to find out what Sadie needs, *turn to page 6.*

If you wave Sadie off with a pleading gesture, *turn to page 7.*

You interrupt Kim to find out what Sadie needs // You try to offer some suggestions to the girls

"You know what, Kim?" you interject. "I really want to be here for you. But give me two seconds to get the girls on the same page. I know it'll buy us more time to talk."

You dart back inside the house to find Elizabeth already glued to her iPad on the couch by herself.

"See?" Sadie admonishes.

"Sorry, Sadie," you offer. "My friend Kim has something on her mind and I got distracted. Let's find something the two of you can play together."

You gather the girls around a small bookshelf filled with toys and games. Some of them have never been opened.

"Have you ladies ever played Twister," you ask.

They shake their heads "no."

"It's super fun," you promise as you unwrap the game and place the colorful mat on the floor. The girls seem interested. "You take turns spinning the spinner and then you get to tell the other person what to do. Like 'left hand on green,'" you demonstrate, careful not to pull a muscle. "You just keep going until the other person falls over," you topple over yourself, just to get a laugh. It works.

"I want to go first," Elizabeth exclaims with a smile on her face.

"Great," you reply. "That means Sadie gets to spin and tell you what to do. And then you just keep going taking turns. Sound good?"

The girls nod. Happy to have some common ground.

"And once you're done taking turns with Twister. We'll take turns doing other stuff," you explain. "Like maybe you color for a bit and then maybe you play dollhouse. We'll just go from there."

You leave Sadie in a good mood, hopeful for a good outcome.

Turn to page 20.

6

You wave Sadie off with a pleading gesture

"Sounds like you guys need a weekend alone," you suggest.

Kim just stares at the trees.

"Or at least a night out. We could take Elizabeth for a sleepover," you offer.

Kim heads downhill fast. "Thanks. But we'd just end up paying for it the next day. She won't sleep a wink in a strange bed."

You try not to take that as an insult. After all, you've been there before and you're just trying to help.

Suddenly, you hear loud THUMPING coming from inside the house. There's GIGGLING, too. So maybe it's not so bad.

"Sounds like they're getting some energy out. That bodes well for some quiet naptime later," Kim muses. "What's new with you?"

If you check on the girls, *turn to page 13.*

If you answer Kim's question, *turn to page 14.*

"Why don't you let us take Elizabeth for a night?" you pose. "You and Jeff could spend the weekend in the city. Just like the good old days."

A thin smile appears on Kim's face. "Remember that time we closed down the Gage and went dancing in Buckingham Fountain?"

"And Jeff tried to outrun those mounted cops?" you chuckle at the thought.

"I had to pull out all the stops to keep them from taking him to jail on horseback," Kim laughs with a lightness returning to her.

And then you notice it. Actually, it's what you don't notice that bothers you. No laughter from inside. No giggling. In fact, the girls are nowhere in sight.

You and Kim search the house, growing more concerned by the minute.

"Sadie!" you call out. "Elizabeth? This isn't funny!"

At last you find them. In the basement playroom. Buried under a pile of dress-ups. Hiding. The room is a complete disaster and Kim doesn't look happy. Her bad day is clearly getting worse.

If you pull the plug and take Sadie home, *turn to page 9.*

If you give Sadie a second chance, *turn to page 12.*

You pull the plug and take Sadie home

"You know what, Kim?" you ask. "I think today just isn't our day."

Sadie can tell by the tone of your voice, she's in trouble. And the long face comes out in force.

"Sadie," you admonish. "Let's clean up these clothes and head home for lunch."

"But I don't want to go," she protests.

Your phone BUZZES in your pocket. More comments to review. Will this day ever get back on track?

"No," you declare. "We're going home. You're having lunch. And then you're taking a nap."

Kim half-heartedly folds the dress-ups. This isn't what she bargained for, but what can you do? After much pouting and shuffling of feet, the girls manage to put the playroom back together and it's time to go.

"I'm sorry, Kim" you proffer. "Can we get together tomorrow for coffee while the girls are in school?"

"Yeah, no," Kim vacillates. "Let me see if I have time after yoga."

You leave Kim's house feeling badly about the ways things went, but sometimes you just can't do it all.

"Can we go shopping for Holly?" Sadie wonders from the backseat.

You catch a glimpse of her hugging her doll in the rearview mirror.

"No, sweetheart," you reply. "Mommy has to work and that playdate didn't go so well."

Sadie just stares out the window, as quiet as she was on the way over.

The End

This may seem like a worse outcome than it actually is. It's true that you were unable to support your friend, you didn't have time to complete your work, and your child played a role in messing up the house. However, she did clean up after herself and learned that even though Elizabeth does not like to play dolls, she does like pillow fights and playing dress-up. The actual lesson from this set of choices is that sometimes you cannot be supportive to your friend, supervise your child, and get all of your work done on the same day. While it would be nice if we could "multi-task" our roles as parent, friend, and employee, the reality is that when we attempt to do three things at once, we end up doing a mediocre job at everything and a good job at nothing. How could it have gone better?

Continued on next page.

1. **Prioritize and Plan Ahead.** What role do you want to ensure you succeed at today, if you can succeed at only one? Do you want to complete your work? Supervise a playdate? Or support your friend? Let's take each role one at a time:

    a. To complete your work, it will be necessary for Sadie to have adequate supervision, and that will require her to play with a friend with whom she has played well before, and whose parent can supervise her adequately. Kim has told you that she is feeling overwhelmed. Therefore, a playdate with Elizabeth being supervised by Kim does not have a high likelihood of resulting in your getting your work completed. A drop-off day care center provides safe, nurturing staff, if there are none of Sadie's friends that are available. Many schools and park districts have drop-in programs for school holidays. Plan ahead. If you know you'll have work to do on a day off from school, make a plan that will allow your child to have fun while you complete your work. Examine the school calendar early (perhaps even over the summer) and plan for those days that you need to simultaneously complete your work and supervise your child(ren).

    b. To support your friend, you'll need to take steps to ensure that Sadie and Elizabeth are playing appropriately. One idea is to drop both of your children off at a Park District program, and delegate supervision to others. However, it's fine to bring Sadie over to Elizabeth and Kim's house. If you choose to do so, you should know that children will inevitably interrupt you while you are having a deep and meaningful conversation. How long could you envision your child behaving appropriately with little or no supervision while on a playdate? Divide that number in half, and set a timer on your phone. Plan to interrupt your conversation with your friend so that you can monitor your child, and praise him or her for good behavior. Would you rather have your conversation or work interrupted by your child's misbehavior, or interrupt the conversation on your terms, at a time you designate, when you could honestly predict a high likelihood that your child is still behaving well? Follow these steps and your chances of an uninterrupted conversation will go up even more:
        • Inform the children of your expectations. Say, "The adults want to talk in the kitchen and we would like you to play nicely, be kind, and be safe."

Continued on next page.

- Create an incentive. Say, "If you're playing nicely, being kind, and being safe when we come into the room to check on you, we'll plan something great to celebrate."
- Allow the children to have some choice in choosing the incentive. Say, "What do you want to do to celebrate?" Avoid anything too extravagant. Good examples are, "We will play a game with you." (attention and time from an adult), "We will jump and do a silly dance." (attention and shared enjoyment with an adult). If it's close to a mealtime, a natural incentive can be choosing the dessert, but food should not be the only type of incentive that is offered.

c. If your primary goal is to supervise the playdate, choose a time when you don't have to simultaneously support your friend and complete your work. Offer to supervise the playdate once your work is finished, and while your friend is getting support from someone else.

You give Sadie a second chance

"Sadie, this isn't what we do when our friends invite us over," you declare.

Sadie looks confused. After all, you told her to have fun and this looks like fun.

"Elizabeth," Kim snaps. "I want this whole room put back together in 5 minutes or this playdate is over. Understand?" Kim bends down to grab a fistful of clothes to shove back in a closet. Elizabeth barely lifts a finger while Sadie cooperates fully.

"Clean it now and I'll give you a cupcake," Kim yells, exasperated. Elizabeth grins, attempting to cash in on the offer by shoving the toys and clothes toward, but not exactly inside, their containers.

Sadie stops cleaning and looks up at you.

"What's wrong, Sadie? Why aren't you cleaning?" you ask.

"Do I get a cupcake, too?" she wonders.

"Let's just worry about playing nicely, okay?" you encourage.

"But we were playing nicely," Sadie explains.

"I know. And that's great. But we need to be able to see you to make sure you guys are safe while you're playing," you reply.

"But this is the playroom!" Sadie protests.

She does have a point.

If you try to convince Kim to hang out a little longer in the playroom, turn to page 18.

If you follow Kim upstairs and let her handle it, turn to page 26.

You check on the girls

You take a peek through the patio door and discover the girls having a pillow fight with the couch cushions. They appear to be having fun, but they're dangerously close to Kim's treasured dollhouse—and possibly on the verge of getting hurt.

"Hang on a sec," you tell Kim before ducking inside her house.

"Hey ladies, I'm glad you're having fun together, but let's try to do something that won't break anything or get you guys hurt," you explain.

You spot several small dolls and small doll pillows in the dollhouse. Remembering that Sadie wants to play dolls, but Elizabeth doesn't like them, you suggest, "Let's see if the dolls can have a pillow fight instead."

You grab two small dolls, name one Veronica and another, Josie, and say, "I'm going to get you, Veronica!" as you make the doll swing the tiny pillow at the other doll.

"Ouch," you squeal in a mousy voice. "Take that, Josie!"

Elizabeth and Sadie start giggling. They take two more dolls and imitate your play fight. And then they start talking through the dolls to create a whole story.

Things seem under control, so you rejoin Kim.

Turn to page 8.

You answer Kim's question

"What's new with me? I've got client comments pouring in all day on a grant that's due tonight," you explain. "And this no school day isn't helping."

"You should have told me," Kim mock scolds you. "I'm happy to have Sadie all day if it helps you get your work done."

It's a tempting offer. Even a few hours might help you catch up. But what about Sadie? Will she feel like you abandoned her high and dry if you leave her with Elizabeth and they don't get along? The GIGGLES grow louder from inside. Something must be going right...

"You know what?" you pose. "I just might take you up on that..."

Suddenly, you hear a loud CRASH!

Elizabeth appears at the door, sobbing.

Turn to page 15.

You both race inside to find Sadie sitting the middle of a crushed dollhouse. Couch cushions are flung all over the place.

"Sadie!" you cry. "What happened?"

Sadie bursts into tears. "She hit me and I fell over."

You collect Sadie in your arms as Kim just stands there in stunned silence. After a few awkward moments Kim mutters with forlorn resignation, "Go to your room, Elizabeth." Elizabeth obeys.

"I'm so sorry, Kim." You bend down to help, but Kim waves you off.

"Another day maybe," Kim offers.

"Really, I..." you interject.

"I'll manage," Kim replies with little conviction.

You grab your things and lead Sadie to the door where the last image you catch is Kim sifting through the broken pieces of her lost childhood.

The End

Clearly, this is a bad outcome. The girls didn't respect their property; they didn't play safely and under control, and Kim's treasured dollhouse was ruined. Kim's stress level increased. You didn't get your work done, and basically everything fell apart. How did this happen?

Continued on next page.

1. **There wasn't one,** but several similar mistakes in judgment. Children often need help to make safe choices that won't result in anyone getting hurt or anything being broken. This is because they are young; not because they are "bad." They don't have the life experience to be able to predict the consequences of their actions. Hence, they make mistakes that are quite predictable. They may bang their head because they stand up straight while crouching under a table. They may get in a pillow fight very close to fragile objects. Each time you had a choice to either supervise the children, or continue talking, you chose to continue talking, despite the girls' repeated demonstrations that they couldn't demonstrate respect and play calmly while unsupervised.

2. **You weren't proactive.** When parents are proactive, they set their children up to succeed, and then retreat into another room to talk. When providing supervision proactively, problems can be anticipated and prevented. Solutions can be taught. Once the children are comfortable, playing safely, and getting along, parents can withdraw confident that their children will be able to sustain their good behavior.

3. **Sadie is at an age when she's choosing her friends** based on their shared interests. She doesn't feel a strong friendship toward Elizabeth because they don't share an interest in dolls. For a child, this is a challenge that requires support to overcome. Instead of offering support and guidance (i.e., stopping the car to determine how Sadie feels and how to find solutions), you continue on auto-pilot assuming everything will be fine, without making much of an effort to increase the probability that it will be.

4. **You didn't communicate your expectations.** There are competing demands on your time and attention throughout this story. You have work to do. Sadie needs supervision and some fun, and your friend, Kim, needs some support. You can only do one thing well at a time. Prior to responding to Kim's text, evaluate your needs and your child's needs, then make a plan. Here are some suggestions:

   a. Communicate: Tell Kim that you have a grant deadline so you won't be able to spend too much time chatting. Listen to Sadie to determine if she would like to spend her afternoon with Elizabeth.

Continued on next page.

b. Plan: Envision how the afternoon should proceed if all of your expectations were met:

- Sadie and Elizabeth will play unsupervised and demonstrate kindness and respect for each other and their property.
- You will get at least 20-30 minutes to speak to Kim.
- You will get at least 60 minutes to work on your grant application.

c. Communicate your expectations to Kim, Elizabeth, and Sadie

d. Provide an incentive to Sadie for cooperating with the plan, and meeting or exceeding your expectations. This could be a tangible reward, or simply a "high five," "huge hug," or 30 minutes of time with you, or (if you are not finished with your work), watching TV. Judge the "value" of the reward based on the amount of effort required for Sadie to meet or exceed your expectations. The more effort required, the more valuable the reward should be.

You try to convince Kim to hang out a little longer in the playroom

"Good point, Sadie," you reply. "There's a lot of fun stuff to do down here."

You step back into the playroom to find Kim closing the door on a closet stuffed with dress-ups.

"Why don't we hang out down here for five minutes?" you suggest. "It's nice and cool and we can start them on an art project."

Kim agrees and you each set the girls up in front of a two-sided easel with some paints before taking a seat on a nearby couch.

"Thanks for coming over today," Kim acknowledges. "I just have to make it through a couple more days."

"You'll get there. I know how hard these days can be with no structure," you reply. "But they seem to be doing okay."

The girls chat away, happily painting.

"I'm making an elephant," Sadie describes.

"Sadie, why don't you ask Elizabeth what she's painting?" you probe.

"What are you painting, Elizabeth?" Sadie blurts out without any hint of the trepidation she showed when she first arrived.

Turn to page 19.

"I'm painting a rainbow. Because my mom loves rainbows!" Elizabeth proudly declares.

Suddenly, Kim softens as a smile finally creeps across her face.

"See," you assure Kim. "I told you you'd get there."

The End

This is a good outcome. Elizabeth shows her loving, kind side of her personality. Sadie and she get along well, and converse with greater ease. In addition, Kim feels less stressed and overwhelmed. How did this happen?

1. **Children often need help to make safe choices** that won't result in anyone getting hurt or anything being broken. This is because they are young; not because they are "bad." They don't have the life experience to be able to predict the consequences of their actions. Hence, they make mistakes that are quite predictable. They may bang their head because they stand up straight while crouching under a table. They may get in a pillow fight very close to fragile objects. Because you provided supervision, offered them choices, and provided them with an opportunity to succeed, the sweet, loving innocence of childhood emerged and warmed the room.

2. **You provided them with support and attention.** By remaining with the girls while they painted, and paying close attention to them, you could facilitate their conversation, promote good choices, and prevent bad ones. Most importantly, you and they could share enjoyment.

For more guidance on positive, proactive parenting strategies, read the afterword.

"How much longer do you think this travel will keep up?" you ask.

"His product launches in January, so it'll be a few more months," Kim explains.

"Sounds like a perfect time for a romantic winter getaway," you suggest. "Maybe back to Tahiti for a honeymoon redux?"

A thin smile appears on Kim's face. "With all of Jeff's miles, it wouldn't cost a dime," Kim muses.

"Might be a good time to get started on number two," you reply.

Kim's smile becomes something else, "Yeesh. After a week like this, I can't even imagine doing it with two kids."

Just then, Elizabeth and Sadie appear at the patio door.

"How was Twister, girls?" you ask.

"Fun!" Sadie blurts.

"But now we want to play dollhouse. Can you help us lift the roof off?" Elizabeth asks with a smile.

You and Kim head inside, happy to assist the girls in the next phase of their playdate. It goes swimmingly as they take turns playing dollhouse, dress-ups, art table, and more. You remind Sadie how proud you are of her efforts to play with Elizabeth.

When the time comes to leave, Sadie begs to stay. Kim offers to keep Sadie a bit longer. And you could use some time to address those client comments, still BUZZING in your pocket.

"All right, Sadie," you concede. "I'll be back in one hour and then it's time to do some shopping for Holly." You give Sadie a wink to let her know that she's done a good job holding up her end of the bargain.

The last thing you hear as Kim closes the door behind you is pure, unadulterated laughter.

The End

This is a fantastic outcome. Sadie and Elizabeth had a great time. You were able to connect with your friend, and you laid the foundation for future successful playdates at Kim's house with Sadie and Elizabeth.

Continued on next page.

They have now acquired the ability to take turns choosing different games to play, and have expanded their repertoire to include games with rules, such as Twister, as well as games of pretend, such as Dollhouse. Finally, you were rewarded with some much-needed time to complete your work. How did it happen?

1. **You took time to listen to your daughter.** She was concerned that she and Elizabeth don't share an interest in playing with dolls. You provided her with some strategies, and also some expectations. You also provided some special incentive to improve her motivation.

2. **You took time to support your daughter** and her friend as they learned to play new games together.

3. **You were open** with Kim when you said you would like to be able to listen carefully to her and be supportive, but you needed to ensure that your children were supported.

4. **You were proactive.** Instead of waiting for problems to arise, you prevented them from arising by spending time initially setting up the girls for success.

You just keep driving

Kim greets you and Sadie at the door with a welcoming smile. "Come in! We're so happy to see you!"

Elizabeth clings to her mother's leg. Shy, but curious.

"Can you say hi, Sadie?" you prompt. Sadie offers a polite wave before Kim leads you into the kitchen for some coffee and bagels. Your phone BUZZES in your pocket, but you try to ignore it. More client comments, tugging on your sleeve.

The girls circle a dollhouse in a playroom just off the kitchen. Unsure of where to start. Kim jumps in, "We brought up my old dollhouse from the basement because I know how much you like dolls, Sadie."

"I don't want to play dolls," Elizabeth protests.

Kim looks embarrassed. Seven days without her husband have taken a toll. It's clear she's barely hanging on and just needs to vent. "Don't be rude," she scolds Elizabeth.

Sadie looks at you with a pained expression that says, "I told you so."

"Shall we?" quips Kim with a sarcastic lilt as she pours you a cup of coffee and leads you out onto the patio.

If you leave the girls to work it out on their own,
turn to page 5.

If you try to offer some suggestions to the girls,
turn to page 6.

You let Sadie play with Elizabeth unsupervised in the basement

"I hope they don't get lost in the piles of laundry," Kim confesses. "It's been really hard to keep up with Jeff away."

Just then, your phone BUZZES. And temptation gets the best of you as you pull it out to sneak a peek at the comments pouring in from your client.

"I don't know how you do it," Kim wonders aloud.

Her voice snaps you out of your zombie haze. "I'm sorry," you offer as you pocket your phone. "These comments are five days late and my deadline hasn't changed," you explain. You take a breath, surveying the kitchen. "Let's make some tea. And I can help you with the dishes. Sound good?"

"Sounds great!" Kim smiles, grateful for the offer.

As you work together, side-by-side, it feels good to help a friend in need. Kim shares her concerns about Jeff's job and the toll it takes on the family. You both long for the simple days—before you measured your lives in square footage and inboxes.

And then the girls show up. Covered in makeup and wearing Kim's bras from the dirty laundry. "Elizabeth!" Kim blurts out, mortified. "Take those off immediately. This was NOT part of the deal."

"But we were bored. There's nothing to do down there," Elizabeth protests.

If you let Kim handle the situation because you think it's not your place,
turn to page 26.

If you interject with an alternative solution,
turn to page 24.

You interject with an alternative solution

"I have an idea, girls," you offer as you swoop in with wet paper towels to remove their makeup. "Let's have a dance party. You get to choose the music and we'll choose some chores to tidy up the house."

"Aww," Elizabeth whines.

"That's no fun," Sadie adds.

"I'm not finished," you improvise. "We'll make teams and have a contest. I'll partner with Elizabeth and Kim will be Sadie's partner."

"What do we win?" Elizabeth wonders, a little more interested than before.

"Whoever makes up the silliest dance gets to be first in line when we dance the Bunny Hop next," you reveal.

"Oh, yeah," Sadie chirps, already shaking her booty.

Kim buys in, too. She grabs her phone and fires up a nearby speaker with some Selena Gomez. The plan works fantastically as everyone moves and grooves to the beats until the house is put back together.

You all go out for ice cream and the girls get along great. Kim is so grateful for the help that she offers to take Sadie and Elizabeth to a movie so you can work on your grant proposal.

The End

This is a great outcome. Your friend, Kim, receives some needed support, the house gets cleaned, and your child has fun. In addition, you get some support from your friend, too, as you are permitted over two uninterrupted hours to finish your work. How did this happen?

1. **You saw an opportunity to provide support** to your child, your friend and her child and you took it. Remember, you are friends with Kim. Would you feel offended if a friend provided support to you at a time when you really needed it, or would you feel appreciative? Her husband is in Hong Kong, you've been friends since college. You didn't hesitate to offer support. Good for you!

2. **You provided guidance** to the children using strategies that include several key factors that improve the probability of success:

Continued on next page.

a. Turn the activity into a game. Even cleaning can be fun if it includes dancing and music (at least it will be more fun than cleaning without dancing and music).

b. Provide an incentive (silliest dance gets to be first in line)

c. Provide attention for cooperative behavior. By joining in the game, you can teach the girls how to clean, and also attend to them while you share the enjoyment of dancing together. Contrast that with, "Clean this basement right now and when it's clean, I'll give you candy." Because you gave them positive attention, and rewarded them with something social (i.e., being first in line) as opposed to something edible, a positive feedback loop was created whereby their cooperative behavior led to shared enjoyment, which led to more cooperative behavior, attention, and praise, and more shared enjoyment. In no time, everyone was having fun and the house was all clean.

3. **You not only supported your friend** by helping the kids to clean the house, you also taught Elizabeth and Sadie how to have fun with each other and their mothers by dancing with them. This expanded Sadie's perspective that the only children with whom she could have fun are those who enjoy playing with dolls. Now, she and Elizabeth share an interest in silly dance contests (and maybe cleaning, too, but I doubt it).

You let Kim handle the situation because you think it's not your place // You follow Kim upstairs and let her handle it

"You know what? Why don't you girls just go play outside?" Kim sighs.

Sadie takes a peek at the overgrown lawn and frowns.

"But the play set is broken," Elizabeth protests once again.

You steal a glance at the rusted-out swings and monkey bars on the rotting wooden structure in the backyard.

"Maybe you can play tag or something?" you offer meekly, more concerned about Kim's fragile mental state.

The girls head outside as you and Kim sit down for some tea at the kitchen table. It isn't long before Elizabeth starts tossing small rocks at the kitchen window. Sadie joins in the fun as well. Eager to annoy you and Kim.

"Remember when we just disappeared on our bikes for the day and our parents had no idea where we went?" Kim muses.

The End

While things could have gone worse, this is a pretty bad outcome. You have not had any time to support your friend. Sadie and Elizabeth clearly are not having "good clean fun," in the way you had hoped. Instead, they are entertaining themselves by annoying you and potentially breaking a window. How did this happen?

1. Let's start with what you can control. Sadie is at an age when she is choosing her friends based on their shared interests. She does not feel a strong friendship toward Elizabeth because they don't share an interest in dolls. For a child, this is a challenge that requires support to overcome. Instead of offering support and guidance, you continue on auto-pilot assuming everything will be fine, without making much of an effort to increase the probability that it will be. Play skills may need to be taught. Instead of assuming your child will just "figure it out," provide "scaffolding" to support your child as she or he learns to play flexibly and functionally.
Want to learn more about improving your child's play skills?
Read the afterword.

2. Once you arrive and discover that your friend, Kim, is overwhelmed, you don't offer support and guidance, but, again, decide to continue on

Continued on next page.   26

auto-pilot assuming that Kim will be able to handle it when all evidence suggests that she is not handling the laundry, housework, or her child's behavior, not to mention that she is concerned about her marriage. Try to empathize with your friend, but remember that your primary responsibility is to ensure your daughter's safety and well-being. If you doubt that your friend is up to the task of providing a safe and enjoyable play opportunity, and you have some ideas that could help, by all means, share them!

3. **What are the signs** that Kim is overwhelmed? Hint: It's not the piles of laundry (though they don't help). Kim is resorting to bribery and threats, rather than support and guidance to increase the chances that acceptable behavior will occur. It takes 2-3 seconds to threaten to punish a child if they don't behave, or bribe them with sweets if they do. In contrast, positive reinforcement, guidance, limits, structure, and support take a little more effort and time, but they pay dividends for months and years to come, across multiple situations and settings.

Want to know the difference between bribery and positive reinforcement? Read the afterword.

You try to urge Elizabeth to come play upstairs

"Do the girls want to play up here?" you ask Kim.

"Only if I get another cupcake," Elizabeth yells from the basement.

Kim just shakes her head and throws her arms up like "What can I do?"

"Fine," Kim replies.

Elizabeth emerges from the basement, takes one look at Holly in Sadie's arms, and announces, "Dolls are for babies!"

Sadie bursts into tears and you pull her aside to explain that Elizabeth is probably unhappy because she misses her daddy.

"I want to go home," Sadie cries.

And, for a second, you want to agree with her. Just then, Elizabeth appears with a cupcake for Sadie.

"I'm sorry," Elizabeth announces. "We can play dolls if that's what you want to do. My mom says we can use my old stroller in the garage."

Sadie grabs the cupcake and smiles.

"Come on," Elizabeth offers. "I'll show you where it is."

Sadie follows Elizabeth to the garage, shoving the cupcake in her mouth.

"Can you tell I've given up?" Kim asks.

If you tell it like it is, *turn to page 29.*

If you smile and fake it, *turn to page 32.*

You tell it like it is

It's true. Kim's your best friend and you just can't beat around the bush.

"How can I help?" you offer.

"You already have," Kim explains. "Elizabeth has been driving me up a wall and I think Sadie will calm her down."

"What about the chocolate and sugar?" you probe. "Do you think that might have something to do with it?"

Kim shakes her head. "Today it's sugar. Tomorrow it's toys. The next day could be clothes," Kim explains. "The longer Jeff's away, the more she won't listen to a word I say."

Your phone BUZZES in your pocket and you can't resist checking it.

"Are you still doing that writing thing?" Kim asks. "God, I wish I had something to distract me like that."

"It's distracting alright," you concede as you scroll through a rapid-fire series of email comments.

The sounds of Elizabeth and Sadie laughing in the garage echo down a long hallway. In fact, they're screeching and screaming.

"Tell you what," Kim suggests. "Why don't you leave Sadie with me for a couple hours and you can get some work done?"

The offer is tempting. A few hours might be just enough time to put out the fires in your inbox. But will Sadie be okay on her own? And how many more cupcakes will she eat before lunchtime?

"Don't worry," Kim promises. "I'll keep them happy."

Who knows what that means? But maybe if you got some work out of the way you could spend quality time with Sadie later.

"Okay," you reply. "But just for a couple hours."

You head for the front door, thanking Kim for helping out.

Turn to page 30.

"Are you kidding?" Kim exclaims. "With Elizabeth off my back, I might be able to make a dent in this mess."

Kim has a point in there somewhere. And you leave with the notion that this may be a mutually beneficial situation.

Until the garage door opens as you back out of the driveway and Sadie waves goodbye with a candy cigarette dangling from her mouth.

The End

This is not a very good outcome. It is hard to feel confident that Elizabeth and Sadie will have fun together for very long, nor do you feel confident that Kim is in a place where she can provide effective supervision.

Nevertheless, Sadie is a girl who makes good decisions most of the time, and you don't allow her too many sugar-filled snacks. So, one afternoon of less structure and supervision with a friend you have known since college is unlikely to create long-term consequences. How could this outcome have been improved?

1. Clearly, you didn't expect Kim to be as overwhelmed as she was. Yet, once you arrived, it is clear that she is. What are the signs that Kim is overwhelmed? Hint: It's not the piles of laundry (though they don't help). Kim is resorting to bribery as a form of parenting and behavior modification. And, as usual, bribery is not working, but, instead, is making

Continued on next page.

Elizabeth's behavior worse. It takes 2-3 seconds to provide a cupcake or a piece of candy to a child; it takes no effort at all, and practically no time. Positive reinforcement, guidance, limits, structure, and support take a little more effort and time, but they pay dividends for months and years to come, across multiple situations and settings.

Want to know the difference between bribery and positive reinforcement? Read the afterword.

2. **Once you arrive and discover** that your friend, Kim, is overwhelmed, you don't offer support and guidance, but, again, decide to continue on auto-pilot assuming that Kim will be able to handle it when all evidence suggests that she is not handling the laundry, housework, or her child's behavior, not to mention that she is concerned about her marriage. Try to empathize with your friend, but remember that your primary responsibility is to ensure your daughter's safety and well-being. If you doubt that your friend is up to the task of providing a safe and enjoyable play opportunity, it may be best to cancel the playdate or stay to supervise it until you have more confidence that it will turn out okay. If you stay for 15 to 30 minutes to ensure a high likelihood of success, you will have more time to complete your work than if you leave knowing the odds are high you'll have to turn around, console your daughter, and resolve a conflict or crisis.

Want to learn more benefits of being proactive to prevent problems before they occur? Read the afterword.

You smile and fake it

"She's probably just going through a phase," you put out there.

"I don't think so. Jeff has her wrapped around his finger," Kim explains. "He gets to bring home gifts from all over, while I'm stuck here playing the bad guy all the time."

The noise from the garage gets louder and louder with Elizabeth and Sadie singing Disney songs at the top of their lungs.

"Elizabeth," Kim calls out. "Why don't you guys bring Holly in here and sing her some lullabies instead? I bet she's tired."

The girls saunter back in the house, reeling from the cupcake sugar high.

"She's not tired!" Elizabeth announces. "She wants to dance!"

The girls leap and sing around the living room, happy to get along, but not exactly well behaved.

The End

This is not a very good outcome for several reasons: 1. You were unable to support your friend. 2. The girls are learning that if they misbehave and act rudely, they will get cupcakes and candy. In short, the children are in control. How could we have improved this outcome?

1. **Power struggles are inevitable** on occasion, but they should not occur frequently. If they do, the adult has the "power" to change the dynamic by adopting the strategy of **shared control**. Shared control consists of a parent or caregiver determining the behavioral expectations for the child but allowing the child some choices. For example, the adults set an expectation that the basement gets clean, and then the children can choose whether they want to clean up the toys first, or the clothes. And, if they do a good job, the children can choose from a "menu" of potential rewards that you have approved (i.e., a high-five, a hug, a tickle fight, or a piggy-back ride).

   To learn more about Shared Control, read the afterword.

2. **True friendships require open and honest communication**, as well as empathy. Clearly, Kim is overwhelmed. When in doubt regarding what to say, start with empathy. Empathy is attempting to guess how another person feels. Say something like, "How are you feeling?" if you don't know the answer to this question, or guess by saying, "You seem very stressed

Continued on next page.

and exhausted. It must feel overwhelming." Simply knowing that your friend "hears" your frustration and can empathize allows those feelings to be acknowledged, which diminishes their intensity. Once emotions are felt less intensely, it is easier to make rational decisions, engage in creative problem solving and listen to suggestions. No one can think rationally when their emotions are overwhelming. It is unlikely that Sadie and Elizabeth will allow you and Kim to have an in-depth conversation that will solve all of her life's difficulties. However, you can offer support and empathy, and schedule a time to discuss her concerns at some point in the near future when you can speak privately.

You ask Sadie what she wants to do

"Can I have a playdate?" Sadie asks enthusiastically.

"With who?"

"Becca!" she screeches.

"Becca who?" you probe with a smile.

You haven't heard Sadie mention Becca before, but, then again, it's only October and you haven't really gotten to know the kids in her class yet.

"She's my friend!" Sadie replies. "We played with the blocks yesterday, remember?"

With your grant work moving at light speed, it's been hard to remember your own name.

"What's her last name, Sadie?" you ask.

"Um, I think it's that place," she replies. "You know."

Oh, boy. This day is going to require some patience, but you remind yourself it's not Sadie's fault that your deadlines are getting tighter by the minute.

"Where you grew up," Sadie finally explains.

"Birmingham?" you wonder.

"That's it!" Sadie jumps up and down.

"Her name is Becca Birmingham?"

"Yes!" Sadie cries. "We laughed about it yesterday."

If you say "Okay," *turn to page 35.*

If you say "Maybe," *turn to page 46.*

You say "Okay"

Sadie dashes to her room faster than you can say "Oka..." while you look up the Birmingham's number in the school directory. There's only one number listed. And you're not sure if it belongs to Becca's mother or father. But you dial it anyway.

An automated voice starts up on the other end as Sadie reappears clutching Bunny, her most cherished and well-loved stuffed animal.

"Hi, it's Sadie's mom." You try to sound natural, but part of you feels weird leaving a message for a stranger. "I realize we haven't had a chance to meet..."

BEEP. Someone's calling through on the other line. The caller ID reads "Adam Birmingham."

"Hello?" you answer, as though you have no idea who's calling.

"Hey, it's Adam," a friendly voice replies on the end. "I just saw you called."

For a split second, you find it odd that someone would call back a strange number before even checking their voicemail, but then you repeat, "Hi, it's Sadie's mom."

"Of course!" Adam exclaims. "We've heard all about Sadie."

Adam 1. You 0. You've probably heard all about Becca, too. But you just weren't listening.

Becca cheers with glee on the other end when Adam lets her know about the playdate. He explains that he also works from home and offers to drop Sadie back at your house just before he picks up his older son from junior high.

"Wow," you reply. "That's 3 hours of uninterrupted work I wasn't expecting. Thanks!"

It's also Sadie's first playdate at a different house you remind yourself. With a new friend. For three hours!

Turn to page 36.

As you drive to Adam's house, you suddenly realize how inexperienced you are as a parent. So many firsts are headed your way.

Becca greets you at the front. All alone behind an unlocked screen door. The two girls quickly disappear into the house as Adam finally appears, taking the girls' excitement in stride.

"Sorry about that," Adam offers. "I was just finishing a call."

After exchanging some basic pleasantries, you decide to ask, "So what will the girls be doing at your house?"

"Oh, you know kids," Adam explains. "They'll just...play. Brian, my oldest, was always making up games on his days off from school."

You nod along, pretending this isn't your first rodeo.

"See you at 3?" Adam prompts.

If you ask to come in, *turn to page 49.*

If you bid Adam farewell, *turn to page 37.*

You bid Adam farewell

You enter your quiet house, happy to have the time to address the comments filling up your inbox. It's not easy working from home, but you've grown to enjoy the flexibility to get the work done on your own time with spaces in between to enjoy your family.

You breeze through the first set of comments faster than you had planned. But now you're stuck waiting on the final set to complete the grant. So, you decide to tackle yesterday's laundry. And as you load the dryer, it happens. Self-doubt starts to creep in.

What if they have a bunch of videogames? *A few hours of video games aren't the end of the world.*

What if Sadie has an accident? *No, she hasn't had one in 2 years.*

Did I see a dog? *Sadie's allergic to dogs.*

Did Adam lock the screen door after I left? *I can't be certain.*

What if Adam doesn't supervise them at all? *Sadie might be in danger!*

The reality is you have no idea who Adam is. You only just met him and now you've entrusted your child with him.

I'm such an idiot!

Why didn't I invite them over to my house? *Wouldn't Adam be the same type of idiot to let Becca come here?*

You check the clock and realize it isn't even 1:00 yet. Two more hours to go. And nothing to do except wait and wonder as the spin-cycle takes over your brain.

I hate laundry!

If you decide to go back to Adam's house, *turn to page 38.*

If you decide to stay put, *turn to page 41.*

You decide to go back to Adam's house

After feeling like either the worst parent because you worry too much, or the worst parent because you don't worry enough, you decide to simply get on your bike and ride the 2 miles back to Adam's house.

Relief sets in when you arrive to find Becca and Sadie outside with sidewalk chalk and Adam nearby with his dog on a leash.

"I decided to check in," you fess up. "I hope you don't mind. I'm still waiting on some final comments and my options were doing laundry or enjoying this beautiful day."

"No problem at all," Adam puts you at ease. "Happy to chat. When Brian was in kindergarten, we made a point to introduce ourselves to every parent. But I guess with your second child, you don't do that as much. Plus, we're just busier now with my wife's practice taking off."

"Practice?" you enquire.

"Amy's a pediatrician," Adam explains. "Do you have any more kids?"

"No, just Sadie," you reply. "For now."

"Becca was our little surprise," Adam explains. "We didn't think we'd be having more little ones, but here she is. Happy and healthy!"

You start to relax. This was a good idea. Sadie would have been fine with Adam, but you would have been nervous. Now, you can relax. Plus, Sadie is having such a good time.

"You wanna see my room?" Becca asks.

"Yeah!" Sadie shrieks and they race back into the house.

"They sure seem to be getting along," Adam says.

Just then your phone vibrates.

Turn to page 39.

"Excuse me," you interject. "This might be the email I was waiting for."

It is. And just as you were starting to get to know this new family.

"I'm so sorry," you offer. "I have to drop these comments into a final draft by tonight."

"Don't worry," Adam assures you. "I got it covered. Or would you rather say goodbye to the girls first?"

After learning your lesson the first time, you reply, "I'll just say a quick goodbye and see what they're up to."

You walk upstairs to discover the beginning of a game that doesn't look very safe. Becca has Sadie's stuffed animal, Bunny, and is throwing it toward the ceiling fan. Sadie looks petrified.

Sadie argues, "It's my turn with Bunny."

"Just one more time," Becca insists.

"No, now. I want Bunny!" Sadie protests.

Becca looks up and sees both you and Adam hovering by the door. She lets Bunny drop to the floor.

"You know, Sadie," you begin. "I think it would be best if I took Bunny home. There are a lot of toys and stuffed animals here, and I wouldn't want you to forget her. You can tell her about your playdate later. I'm sure she'll be excited to hear all about it when you get home."

Sadie rolls her eyes. A skill she's mastering far too quickly.

"Mommy," Sadie scolds. "Bunny can't hear me. Stop pretending."

Sadie agrees to let you take Bunny home. You hug and kiss her goodbye and thank Adam again for having her.

"I'll have Sadie back at 3 on the dot," Adam promises.

"Perfect!" you reply.

As you pedal home on your bike, you take comfort in knowing that your daughter is safe and happy, your work will get done, and you'll still have some quality time left for your family.

The End

This is a great outcome. How did you do it?

Continued on next page.

1. **You trusted your instincts** Even though it turned out to be foolish to worry, your own gut told you that you felt uncomfortable dropping Sadie off with a family you hadn't gotten to know yet. Once you acquired your own peace of mind, you were free to trust some additional instincts—to check on Sadie one more time before going home.

2. **You prevented future problems by being proactive.** Even though nothing had gotten broken yet, you realized that the following were "red flags" that were the sign of possible trouble in the near future:

   a. Becca and Sadie were arguing over Bunny

   b. They were throwing objects into a ceiling fan

   What could possibly go wrong? You answered that question for Sadie and from Sadie's perspective by saying, "There are a lot of toys and stuffed animals here, and I wouldn't want you to forget her." By spending just a couple of minutes monitoring and providing some guidance, you were able to prevent a problem from arising.

3. **In addition, you were authentic and open with Adam.** Sadie is your first child. You are a beginner. Adam validated your actions by recalling that he, too, took time to get to know his first child's friends and their parents, and he appreciated having the time now to do so again with Becca's friends. Authenticity is a great way to form a friendship, and it allows for genuine understanding.

You decide to stay put

You move to the kitchen for some mineral water with a hint of ginger. That usually calms you down. Are these feelings rational? You wonder. It's not exactly the day you expected it was going to be, but Sadie has become an independent, charismatic, little girl with her own ideas about how she spends her time.

As the ginger hits your palette, you're struck by a feeling akin to an earthquake inside your stomach. You remember a story you read last week on Facebook called "Who are the people in your neighborhood?" with a link to the sex offender registry.

In a panic, you race back to your laptop, find the link, and type in "Adam Birmingham." No results found. The earthquake subsides. You check the clock and realize you've still got 90 minutes to go. Enough time for a yoga class? Maybe.

As you scroll through a list of classes online, hoping for an opening that works...PING. The email you've been waiting for comes through with the subject line: "NEED THIS IN 2 HOURS!"

Turn to page 42.

This is it. Time to dive in headfirst. And a great way to keep your mind focused on something other than Sadie and the misadventures she may or may not be having. You set your phone aside and pound away at the keyboard. Time flies and the tension in your spine eases with each comment you knock down. Who needs yoga anyway?

An hour later, you're in great shape. Just one final proofread and you'll be ready to hit "send."

And then you remember your phone. The one sitting next you. Face down. On mute. You flip it over and find a text from Adam: "Please call. Not an emergency."

Your worst fears trample your rational expectations as you dial Adam's phone.

"The girls had a bit of a conflict," Adam explains. "Nobody was hurt, but Becca accused Sadie of pulling her hair and Sadie won't speak to me."

"Can you put Sadie on the phone, please?" you request.

After a brief pause you hear her meek voice, "Can you come pick me up?"

"Is everything okay?" you enquire. "What happened?"

"Just come get me," Sadie implores.

Adam explains that it has something to do about a bunny, but it didn't make much sense to him. You check the clock. Just 30 more minutes and you'll be home free. The grant will be finished and you'll have the rest of the day to spend with Sadie.

If you decide to work for a few more minutes, *go to page 43*.

If you decide to go straight to Adam's, *go to page 54*.

You decide to work for a few more minutes

Phew. It was just the bunny. Not so big a deal. You promise Sadie that you'll be there soon. I bet I could finish this work in 15 minutes if I simply avoid looking at my phone, you tell yourself. Maybe they'll even work it out on their own before you get there. You tell Adam you'll be there in 20 minutes, but it takes closer to 45 before you make it to his door. He doesn't look happy.

"Sadie, your mom's here," Adam calls out.

Sadie walks quietly to the front door while Adam ties Becca's shoes. You mouth the words to Adam, "Did it get any better?" Adam shakes his head as he quickly rushes Becca out the door along with you. And then you see the 2 texts and 3 missed calls from Adam and remember...

"Oh, no!" you exclaim. "Your son. I'm so sorry."

"It's okay," Adam lies. "I texted the school. He knows I'm late."

SLAM go the car doors. On the ride home, Sadie asks to watch a DVD.

"It's only a short drive home," you explain. "How was your playdate?"

No response from Sadie. Maybe she's tired or hungry. You don't push it.

You arrive home and Sadie goes straight to her room without speaking to you.

Two minutes later, Sadie appears in the hallway, balling.

"What's wrong, honey?" you ask.

"Mommy! Bunny is still at Becca's!" she sobs.

You lift her up and hug her close.

"We can go back and get Bunny. It's okay," you explain.

"No, it's not okay," Sadie protests. "Becca said she wasn't going to give her back. She took Bunny!" Sadie is inconsolable now. Trembling even.

After what seems like an eternity, Sadie finally calms down and you make it to your phone and dial Adam.

"Sorry, I can't talk right now. I'm just pulling up in front of Brian's school," Adam explains.

"No problem. I was just wondering..."

"Can I call you back in 10 minutes?" Adam interrupts.

Turn to page 44.

You make a grilled cheese for Sadie before pacing the kitchen like a prisoner awaiting sentencing. Adam finally calls back to offer more color on the playdate.

"I think it started with Becca pulling on some bunny ears. And then Sadie may have pulled on Becca's hair," Adam explains.

"Well, Sadie can get pretty territorial about her stuffed animals, especially Bunny," you offer. "I'm so sorry this didn't work out."

"Hey, sometimes kids don't get along," Adam concedes. "It's okay."

"By the way, I think Sadie left her bunny at the house, can I stop by to pick it up?" you probe.

"I'm sorry, but no one's home," Adam declares. "I'm with Becca on the way to my parents so they can babysit."

"All right then," you concede. "It's just that..."

"Sorry, this is a work call," Adam interjects. "I gotta go. I'll pack the bunny in Becca's backpack for tomorrow. Bye."

You anxiously approach Sadie, knowing full well what's at stake. Sadie has slept with Bunny every night of her life. Not one night without her precious, well-loved stuffed animal.

"Sadie?" you mutter in a sheepish tone, one that Sadie sniffs out in a heartbeat.

She looks up from her grilled cheese and the tears start to flow even harder than before.

The End

Wow, you really blew it this time. You disappointed your daughter, lost her prized bunny, inconvenienced Adam, and rushed through your work. Sadie and Becca may work out their differences during school, but Adam will remember you as "the flake" who doesn't answer her phone or texts when her daughter's been crying. How could this have gone better?

Continued on next page.

44

1. Start by being proactive. When you realize that Sadie is going over to a new house for the first time, try to envision all of the times when Sadie had a successful playdate. What did she do? What contributed to its success? Did she share? Did she take turns? Did they play a particular game? Did you stay and play with her for a few minutes to ensure she was playing nicely? Once you've identified the key ingredients that have led to successful playdates in the past, **communicate** those to Sadie and to Adam. Tell Sadie, "You know, you've had great playdates in the past when you've shared, used manners with the adults, and a grown up helps you get started on a game. Do you think you could do that while you're at Becca's house?" With Adam, you could say, "This is Sadie's first time at your house. Do you think either you or I could watch them for a few minutes when they get started so that she is comfortable?

2. Envision what has led to unsuccessful playdates in the past. Or, if you haven't had any playdates previously, try to imagine what are some realistic, likely pitfalls that may interfere with a successful playdate. Has Sadie ever been territorial with her bunny? Would she be very upset if she forgot Bunny at Becca's house, or some place they visit, like the park? If so, leave Bunny at home!

3. Finally, set a goal with Sadie. Be specific and positive. Ask her, "What's the most important thing to remember while at someone else's house?" Regardless of the words she uses, there are always 2-3 things: Be safe. Be kind. Cooperate. These words are more powerful than, "Don't hit." "Don't be rude," or "No arguing." By choosing **positively-worded** expectations, Sadie will be encouraged to do more than refrain from negative behavior; she will hear what behaviors you expect her to demonstrate. Besides, it is hard to be genuinely proud of your child for going 3 hours without hitting someone. Compare that to how proud you would be if Adam told you, "Sadie was so kind and cooperative."

You say "Maybe"

"Maybe," you reply, knowing that Sadie won't be satisfied with that answer.

"Please!" Sadie screeches.

"Sadie, I would love for you to have a playdate with Becca, but I don't know her or her family. And, you've never had a drop-off playdate before. Let's talk about it."

"Call her. Call her!" Sadie isn't interested in a deep and meaningful conversation. Your six-year-old simply wants to play with her friend—NOW!

You're proud of Sadie for making friends so quickly, but you know she still has a way to go when it comes to sharing. And, come to think of it, her friends aren't very good at sharing, either. Sometimes you feel more like a referee than a parent. And, you have a deadline on that grant application. How are you going to host a playdate, referee conflicts, and get work done?

"Okay, let me look up Becca's parents' names and their address and phone number. We need to be really nice to their family because we haven't made plans with them before," you explain.

"Hello, this is Adam," a friendly voice greets you on the other end.

"Hi, it's Sadie's mom," you reply. "Apparently, my daughter and your daughter, Becca, play together at school."

There's an awkward pause on the line. Followed by some muffled whispers. It sounds like "Becca...someone named Sadie...from school." You start to wonder if you've dialed the wrong number and then, suddenly, you hear shrieks of excitement.

Adam comes back on the line. "Yes, apparently they do." He seems a bit distracted. "I have some conference calls coming up, but I'm always looking for someone to keep Becca occupied."

It's not exactly the warmest invitation, but you understand where he's coming from. Plus, he offers to drop Sadie back off at your house when he goes to pick up his son from junior high. Bingo!

Turn to page 47.

"Sadie, good news! Becca is free," you announce. "But..." You pause to ensure that Sadie is paying attention. Instead, she bolts to her room and returns clutching her well-loved stuffed animal, Bunny. Hmm. This might be a problem.

"Sadie, we have to make a plan," you announce as she bounces in her shoes with excitement.

You drop down to her eye level and hold her hand to say succinctly, "Sadie, you're so fun to play with. Your friends and I always giggle when we play."

Sadie smiles and nods.

"Sometimes, the fun ends when you don't share, or they don't share with you," you caution. "I have a feeling that it will be very hard for you to share Bunny. And, I bet Becca has a toy or stuffed animal that she loves just as much as you love Bunny. She'll probably find it very hard to share that, too."

Sadie responds, "Oh, she does! She brings her pig, Olivia, to school and the teacher tells her to keep it in her cubby."

"What would happen if I went to her house and grabbed Olivia without asking first?" you ask.

"She would cry," Sadie replies confidently.

"Do you think you can avoid grabbing Olivia, especially without asking first?" you probe.

"Sure, don't tell Becca, but I think Olivia is scary," Sadie admits. "She has all of these whiskers and her eye is about to fall off."

"Okay, then that'll be easy," you explain. "It's very important that you're kind and patient with Becca. This is your first time to her house. So, use your best manners, and let her choose the first game. You can choose the second game. Take turns! Same goes for sharing..."

Sadie is starting to look bored. You need to wrap this up. "So, what are you going to do to make this the most fun day with Becca?" you ask enthusiastically.

Turn to page 48.

"Play and eat ice cream!" she exclaims, obviously not taking in the lesson you thought you had conveyed so clearly.

"Well, you certainly will play, but I want you to share, be kind, use manners and take turns," you explain. "Can you repeat that?"

"Use manners and take turns."

"That's right, and also be kind, okay?" Maybe your list was a bit too long to remember, but she's doing a great job.

"And then we get ice cream?" Sadie wonders.

"Actually, that's not a bad reward. If you share, take turns, and use manners."

"Deal," she announces with delight.

You shake hands playfully and walk Sadie to the door where Adam and Becca greet you with a smile. The girls disappear in a heartbeat, laughing and giggling.

"See you at 3?" Adam asks as he checks his email on his phone.

If you ask to come in, *turn to page 52.*

If you bid Adam farewell, *turn to page 57.*

You ask to come in

"Actually, do you mind if I stick around for a few minutes?" you ask. "It's Sadie's first playdate away from home and I just want to make sure she's comfortable before I take off."

"No problem at all," Adam assures you, still distracted by his email. "I remember doing the same thing when our son, Brian, was little."

Adam's saying the right things, but you wonder how present he's going to be with his work distractions. And the girls are nowhere to be found. Suddenly, Sadie appears in tears.

"Yes!" Adam exclaims. Pumping his phone in his fist. Uh, hello?

"What is it, honey?" you ask Sadie while Becca hovers nearby. Sadie won't talk, but she has tears in her eyes.

Adam explains, "My call got pushed until tomorrow."

Becca runs to her dad and announces, "Sadie pulled my hair!"

Oh, boy. Not what you wanted to hear. "Let me speak to Sadie in another room, if you don't mind." You're firm in your resolve, but mortified that the first time you meet this family, this is what you're dealing with.

"What happened?" you demand. Sadie starts to curl into a ball on the chair, clutching Bunny. She's not looking at you. You soften your voice, speak quietly and say, "Sadie, honey. You need to tell me what happened. Becca's daddy said you pulled Becca's hair. Did you?" No response.

You meet Adam back in the foyer, apologize for Sadie's behavior, and announce that the playdate is over.

"Would it be okay if I try to speak to Sadie?" Adam wonders. "I talked to Becca and I suspect there's more to the story."

Relieved by the marked turnaround in Adam's focus, you see no harm.

"Sadie, I know you don't know me very well, and I don't know you very well either," he admits. "Do you normally pull your mom's hair?"

Sadie smiles at how silly that question sounds, but she still isn't talking. "Sadie, what happened right before you and Becca started arguing?" he asks.

"We were playing," Sadie reveals. "And then she took Bunny and pulled her ears."

Turn to page 50.

49

You interrupt, "Bunny is Sadie's favorite stuffed animal. She takes her everywhere. What happened next, Sadie?" Your anger builds as you ask a question to which you think you already know the answer.

"Nothing!" Sadie replies unconvincingly.

Adam asks, "Did you ask Becca to give Bunny back?"

"Yes, but she wouldn't," Sadie explains. "So, I grabbed it and then she cried."

Adam turns to Becca, "Did you give Bunny back to Sadie when she asked for her?"

"No, she pulled my hair before I could give it back," Becca explains.

"I didn't!" Sadie protests.

"Did, too! You grabbed my hair just as I was deciding to give her back to you," Becca argues.

Adam turns to you in hushed tones, "I've seen this 1000 times before with her brother. Becca held the bunny next to her head. And Sadie probably pulled 1 or 2 hairs accidentally when she grabbed it back. But let's play along."

Based on your first impression, you wouldn't have guessed Adam was such an experienced parent. Having two kids must have something to do with it. You make a mental note for the future and let Adam take the lead.

Turn to page 51.

He turns to Becca, "Is there any chance that she only pulled a couple of your hairs?"

"No. She pulled 4. I counted," Becca answers.

"Is your head okay now?" Adam asks.

"Uh huh," Becca reveals.

"Can you say 'sorry' to each other?" Adam prompts.

The two kids mumble "sorry" and walk downstairs to the basement. Within two minutes, the problem is over. Adam offers you some coffee.

The End

This is a great outcome. You met a great dad. Sadie and Becca resolved their argument, and you are in a position to have a wonderful rest of the day. How did you do it?

1. **You trusted your instincts** It's understandable to feel less than comfortable when dropping your child off at the home of a family you don't know very well. You stayed long enough to form more than a first impression. You stayed until you were comfortable. And, you turned out to be more than just comfortable; you were impressed by Adam's parenting skills. There are many challenges in parenting that are not covered in the stack of parenting books gathering dust on your bedside stand. Sometimes, you just need to hear and see the voice and actions of an experienced parent.

2. **You trusted Adam to intervene,** and monitored how he did so. Adam is an experienced parent. Becca is his second child. He may have a larger bag of tricks than you do. How do you fill your bag with similar tricks? Watch skilled parents and imitate them. Now, it's possible that your child's friends don't have parents as skilled, patient, and experienced as Adam. This is why it is important to monitor your child's friends' parents before you entrust your child with them.

3. **You were prepared to end the playdate,** but willing to listen and consider other options before making a final decision. Good parents are firm, but fair. Given the actual facts regarding the situation, it would not have been fair to end the playdate immediately. Yet, you responded swiftly and fairly, and remained at Adam's house to continue to monitor how the two girls got along.

You ask to come in

"I was wondering if I might be able to just come in for a second?" you ask. "It's Sadie's first playdate away from home and she can be a little territorial about sharing."

Adam puts down his phone, aware of his need to be present and focused.

"No problem at all," he assures you. "Please come in. Our son, Brian, had the same issues when he was little. Can I get you some coffee?"

You check your watch and think of your deadline. A few minutes won't set you back too much. Plus, it's a perfect chance to get to know a new family.

"Sure," you reply.

As you and Adam tiptoe up the stairs, you discover a bedroom that's been converted into a magical land with ponies in a line, sheets made into a tent, and the shadows of two little girls making their ponies talk to each other under the fort that they've created.

"I love you, Pinky Pie," Sadie says in a squeaky voice.

"Then marry me, Brown Clydesdale," replies Becca.

The girls catch you spying when they peek out of the tent to arrange the horses for the wedding ceremony.

"Mr. Birmingham, will you get some flowers?" Sadie asks.

"Sadie," you interject. "Remember our deal?" You pantomime eating ice cream.

Turn to page 53.

"Please, Mr. Birmingham?" Sadie smiles.

Adam puts his hands in a fist, creating an invisible bouquet of flowers and hands them to Sadie. The game continues as your phone vibrates. But you ignore it to take in the sights and sounds of 6-year-olds in their own, magical world.

The End

This is a fantastic outcome.
How did you do it?

1. **You were proactive.** Prior to agreeing to the playdate, you communicated your expectations. The way you communicated them followed a tried and true formula:

   a. You started with something positive and true (you giggle and enjoy playdates).

   b. You introduced the problem that you are trying to solve (sometimes sharing is difficult).

   c. You communicated your expectations using positive examples (share, take turns, use manners).

   d. You ensured she understood the expectations.

   e. You agreed on an incentive/ reward.

2. **You provided supervision.** You didn't simply drop her off and hope for the best. You monitored Sadie and Becca's play. You were present and free from the distractions of your phone. For the five to ten minutes you were in Becca's house, you chose to ignore your phone and observe the magical world created by Sadie and Becca. These tender moments are the treasures of childhood. Because you invested just a small amount of time, you were rewarded with a treasured memory.

You decide to go straight to Adam's

"I came over as soon as I could," you announce, still a bit stressed by the drive.

The girls are in the kitchen, but they're not speaking. Sadie cries softly. Becca tries not to make eye contact. It might be cute and a bit humorous if your little girl didn't look so upset.

Adam begins, "Sadie's bunny has a problem."

Sadie can't stand it anymore and runs to your lap. She buries her head in your chest and acts as helpless and miserable as a newborn who can't find her pacifier.

"What happened?" you ask earnestly.

"Well, I'm not quite sure," Adam admits. "But the end result is that Bunny will need some surgery. Becca, can you please tell Sadie's mom what happened?"

Becca begins, "We were playing a really fun game. At least, I thought it would be fun, and um, the fan shot Bunny into the other room. We ran to get her and couldn't find her for a while."

Sadie interrupts, "I told you we should have shot Olivia into the other room, but you shot Bunny. Bunny doesn't like to be hit in the head!"

Adam retrieves a bunny from the other side of the room. And it's missing one ear.

"Oh my goodness!" You're shocked to see the love of Sadie's life, a once soft, cuddly toy, reduced to a one-eared bunny with a shredded head.

"Sadie, we can fix this," you manage to say with some conviction and authority that you don't genuinely possess.

"We can?" Sadie asks.

Becca and Adam, too, are amazed by your apparent confidence.

"Sure. But, it won't be easy. I will try my hardest. Bunny may not ever be exactly the same, but I will promise you that I will try very hard to fix Bunny. Okay?"

Sadie nods. Unsure. So, you kneel down next to her.

Turn to page 55.

"Sadie, I love you and I know that you love Bunny. It was an accident, and it's okay to be sad," you advise. "Can you try to enjoy the rest of your time with Becca while I take Bunny home and figure out the best way to perform surgery on a bunny?"

Your optimism strikes a chord in Sadie that gives her security and strength.

Becca whispers something into Adam's ear. Adam nods. Becca walks up to Sadie and hands her an adorable, well-loved, slightly stained stuffed dog. She says sweetly, "Sadie, you can sleep with Bear tonight."

Sadie hugs Bear and Becca. You get a little misty-eyed.

"Sadie, I'm going to go home now," you explain. "Try to have fun and I'll see you later, okay?"

"Okay, Mommy. Bye," she smiles.

The End

This is a pretty good outcome, given that you made the best of a difficult situation. Sometimes, the best you can do is be honest. Bunny won't be exactly the same again, but Sadie will also not be the only child on Earth who sleeps with a one-eared stuffed animal. In the grand scheme of things, this is not a crisis, and you are supporting your child the best you can, while not overreacting. Children take their cues from the adults around them whom they trust. Most parents watch their toddlers tumble as they learn to walk. The first thing the little boy or girl does after their fifth or sixth fall of the day is look around to see if anyone was watching. If no adult makes eye contact with them, many times, the toddler doesn't even cry. Sure, it hurts, but they may reason, it couldn't be a crisis because no one is rushing over and no one else is that upset. Even as adults, athletic trainers, EMT's, and ER doctors and nurses stay quite calm during crises. Anxiety does not help a situation, but calm, rational confidence that the situation will be handled usually starts a very positive process of recovery and resilience. So, what specifically did you do correctly?

1. **You trusted** that most parents would not take the extraordinary step of calling you unless the problem, in their judgment, required your attention and effort. In response to this phone call, you prioritized your child's needs. By spending time with Sadie now, it allowed you to assess the situation, offer the best solution you could, and then return to your second priority, work.

Continued on next page.

What could you have done better?

1. **Start by being proactive.** When you realize that Sadie is going over to a new house for the first time, try to envision all of the times when Sadie had a successful playdate. What did she do? What contributed to its success? Did she share? Did she take turns? Did they play a particular game? Did you stay and play with her for a few minutes to ensure she was playing nicely? Once you've identified the key ingredients that have led to successful playdates in the past, communicate those to Sadie and to Adam. Tell Sadie, "You know, you've had great playdates in the past when you've shared, used manners with the adults, and a grown up helps you get started on a game. Do you think you could do that while you're at Becca's house?" With Adam, you could say, "This is Sadie's first time at your house. Do you think either you or I could watch them for a few minutes when they get started so that she is comfortable?"

2. **Envision** what has led to unsuccessful playdates in the past. Or, if you haven't had any playdates previously, try to imagine what are some realistic, likely pitfalls that may interfere with a successful playdate. Has Sadie ever been territorial with her bunny? Would she be very upset if she forgot Bunny at Becca's house, or some place they visit, like the park? If so, leave Bunny at home.

You bid Adam farewell

You arrive at home after a two-mile drive that filled you with a mix of emotions. Sadie was very excited to play with Becca, but why didn't I stay to make sure the house is safe and they get along? You reassure yourself. There is a first time for everything. This is Sadie's first playdate at Becca's house. Why do I feel nauseous?

If you decide to turn around, *turn to page 58.*

If you decide to stay home, *turn to page 60.*

You decide to turn around

After feeling chagrined for abandoning your child at a house you didn't even bother to step inside, and with a man you could barely recognize, you turn the car around with newfound conviction. Leaving the car parked at an odd angle in front of Adam's house, your confidence wanes as you ring the bell. You take a deep breath and smile nonchalantly as Adam looks at you inquisitively through the screen.

"I'm sorry for rushing off before," you say, realizing that this isn't exactly what happened.

Still puzzled, Adam replies, "That's okay, the girls are in back. Is everything okay?"

"Yes, it's just...well...I don't know you very well and Sadie has never been here before. Do you mind if..."

"Oh, of course, don't be silly. Stick around as long as you like. You can never be too careful these days. I'm always walking Becca to school now that her brother, Brian, is too embarrassed to be seen with me," Adam confesses. "When did giving your dad a hug turn into a half-hearted side-wave and a look behind him to make sure no one saw him?"

Adam seems normal. That's a good sign. Perhaps I didn't need to panic and rush right back over, you reassure yourself. But still. "Where are the girls, Adam?"

"Out back. I'll show you," Adam explains.

You spot a rotted, wooden play set that looks like it could blow over if someone sneezed too closely to it. The girls are walking towards it as Adam boasts, "I built the swing set 10 years ago with some scrap wood that was in the garage when we bought the house."

He leans on the swing set. You hear a crack. Adam pulls his hand back quickly, examining a 1-inch sliver sticking out of his hand. Embarrassed, he takes a few steps backwards.

Becca rolls her eyes at her father. "Daddy, now can we get a new swing set? You said once this one falls over..." Adam laughs at himself. He turns sideways to you. "Do you think I could get a new one installed before my wife gets home?"

"I don't know about that, but I'm sure we could have some fun knocking this one over before she gets home," you offer.

Adam smiles as he responsibly says, "Girls, I'm sorry, but this play set has to be off-limits until I can safely get rid of it. Want to draw with sidewalk chalk while I get some snacks ready?"

You offer to help with the snacks and learn more about Adam. His wife is a pediatrician. He stays home to watch the kids. He asks about your work and

Turn to page 59.

shows genuine interest. You walk outside once the snacks are ready and you find Sadie proudly finishing a multi-colored family of stick figures that are all standing near a swing set.

"Mommy, this is Becca's family working with us to build a new play set," she announces with pride.

"I drew a unicorn, Daddy," interrupts Becca

You walk behind Sadie and whisper, "Thank you for playing so nicely. I'm going to enjoy having ice cream with you later."

Sadie smiles proudly and gives you an unsolicited hug that warms your insides. Do I really only get six more years of these hugs before she is embarrassed to see me? You wipe that thought out of your mind as you hold her small hand inside yours and walk inside.

The End

This is a good outcome, even though there were some close calls. What did you do right?

1. **You started by being proactive.** You made a plan with Sadie prior to starting the playdate. She knew you were expecting her to play nicely, use manners, and share. She knew that you would be proud of her, and she would earn ice cream. You set her up for success before the playdate even started.

2. **You trusted your instincts.** Anxiety is not always bad. Some anxiety serves as a signal of potential danger. While you had no way of knowing there was an unsafe play set in Adam's house, the anxiety you felt did signal that you had left Sadie before you had any evidence that she would be safe and happy at Becca's house. So, you summoned the courage to confront the small amount of awkward feelings that arose when you returned. This allowed you to be genuine and open about why you were returning to Adam and Becca's house.

3. **You provided supervision** while the children played. This permitted you to see the destruction of the play set, and prevent anyone getting injured.

4. **You "caught Sadie being good."** Because you had previously agreed on a set of expectations and a reward, your brief whisper in Sadie's ear alerted her to a powerful positive message: I notice you making good decisions, and I am proud of you. Plus, you can trust that when I make a deal with you, I will follow-through and enjoy celebrating your success. Shared enjoyment strengthens attachments, provides powerful feelings of self-efficacy, and, when paired with specific, labeled praise contributes to the foundation for self-esteem.

You decide to stay home

Quit being a "helicopter parent," you admonish yourself. You don't need to follow every paranoid recommendation that you read on Facebook. Or do you? You message a couple friends about Adam Birmingham and no one has any info as they are new to the school district. You manage to quell the panic stirring just beneath your skin as you check the clock. Over two hours before this playdate ends. You open your email and see 14 separate messages titled, "Grant revisions." I guess those reviewers finally read your latest draft. Time to get to work.

Sixty minutes fly by as you start to make a dent in your workload. You check your phone. No messages. See, no need to worry. As if on cue, your phone rings. Not a text message, a voice call. You recall the number is Adam Birmingham's.

"Hello?" you answer.

"There's been an accident," Adam announces. "I'm so sorry. Sadie is hurt and we need to take her to get an x-ray. I think she may have broken her arm."

"What?!" you shriek. "Okay. I'll be right over." Without hanging up, you grab your keys, get in the car, and keep talking to Adam.

"Our old play set has some monkey bars," Adam explains. "I was inside making snacks so I didn't see exactly how it happened, but I've got some ice on her arm and it's already turning black and blue. I feel awful."

You arrive at the Birmingham's in less than five minutes. Sadie tries to hug you, but stops abruptly with a yelp. She starts wailing. Your heart aches as you experience her pain with her.

Turn to page 61.

Out of the corner of your eye, you see a decrepit play set that looks 50 years old with several cracks on it. In the kitchen, you notice a very large Ziploc bag of oregano. Or is that...? Yep, you catch the pungent smell of marijuana coming off Adam as he hands you a fresh bag of ice. As you turn back towards Sadie, you spy a handgun on the kitchen table.

No time for goodbyes!

You get Sadie buckled into her booster seat and blaze a trail to the ER.

At first, you thought the worst thing you had done was to forget to bring Bunny to console her. Now, you realize there were more important things you forgot to do. How could I have been so stupid to not even walk through the threshold of the front door when I dropped Sadie off? Traffic on the way to the ER is making the worst day of your life even worse.

At the ER, Sadie explains that she was crossing the monkey bars and one of the bars just broke in her hands. She fell and started crying. How do monkey bars just break under the weight of a tiny girl? Why didn't I stay at Adam's?

The End

This could be the worst outcome possible. I hope you learned some lessons. What could you have done differently?

1. **Before dropping off your child** in a new environment, it is always important to take a look around. While accidents happen, it would be important to know whether this accident could have been prevented. Not knowing adds insult to injury, as you cannot console yourself with the knowledge that you did everything you could. You felt anxious about leaving Sadie, but you ignored your feelings. In the future, **trust your instincts.**

2. **The most challenging aspect** of parenting is not the decisions you make with your own child, but being unable to control your children's friends' parents and their decisions. How do you judge someone else's parenting skills? The reality is, you can't. The best you can do is look for obvious signs of trouble. What can you assess?

    a. Is the parent going to supervise the children?

    b. Is the physical environment safe for children?

    c. Do they have weapons in the home?

    d. Are they stored safely?

    e. Are there any recreational drugs lying around the kitchen table?

Continued on next page.   61

3. You might not have time to truly get to know every one of your child's friends and their parents, but you should make time to have an introductory conversation. Unlike childcare centers and schools, you don't need to pass a background check to become a parent or host a playdate. What are some basic pieces of information you should obtain?

   a. What is the best way to reach him/her during the playdate?

   b. Where will they be (at home, a park, a restaurant)?

   c. If a nanny or other caregiver will be watching the children, could you meet them, or get their contact information?

   d. In the US especially, are there any firearms in the home? If so, are they locked and stored safely?

While this information should be assessed, it is not imperative to "interview" each parent, but casually enter the home, observe the surroundings, and demonstrate genuine curiosity and concern for your and their child's safety. Ninety-nine percent of parents are trying their best and share your concern about children's welfare. If you happen to encounter a member of the 1% of parents who are not capable of supervising a playdate safely, these basic safeguards may prevent a serious injury or crisis.

Afterword—Notes from the expert

Be Proactive

How often have we heard that hindsight is 20-20? Attempting to engage in foresight is actually much more powerful than trying to learn from the past. Prior to making a decision, try to envision what your child would need to do for the upcoming situation to go well. What would a positive outcome look like, in your opinion? What would it look like in your child's opinion? Having a shared vision or goal will align yourselves with one another and increase the likelihood that the goal will be achieved.

Part of the planning process also allows you to agree on the contingencies. How will you react if your child meets or exceeds your expectations? How will you react if he or she does not? Planning ahead of time prevents rash and impulsive decisions. Agreeing on a shared goal prevents miscommunication and allows for joint problem solving. By the end of the day, you will end up spending an equal amount of time talking to your child about each important event they encounter. Would you rather spend 5 minutes planning for how to prevent difficulties, promote desirable behavior, and celebrate success, or spend 5 minutes explaining why you were disappointed by their behavior when they did not meet your expectations? It's your 5 minutes, spend them how you wish. But you will be happier with the outcome if you spend the time prior to important events trying to prevent mistakes and promote good decisions.

When Sadie asks for a playdate, saying "maybe" allowed you to set some expectations, and also agree on a reward for meeting or exceeding those expectations. If Sadie shares and uses manners, you could celebrate with ice cream. Also, you could easily imagine a situation that may make sharing difficult (i.e., being asked to share her favorite stuffed animal), as well as situations that may make future events difficult (i.e., forgetting the bunny, or getting it stuck in a fan). Prevention is key. Leave the valuable objects at home—problem solved because you prevented it from occurring.

Friendships

When do children distinguish between children with whom they spend a lot of time, and actual friends? Typically, children in preschool and kindergarten (under age 6) will play with anyone who seems to be approximately the same age as them and with whom they are familiar.

You may notice kindergarten teachers saying, "Friends, please sit down." In practice, adults determine who will be a child's playmate at these young ages. Around first grade (age 6-7), children start to distinguish between which peers share interests with them, and which ones do not. They make decisions regarding whom they wish to spend time outside of school. These decisions, like many they make at that age, may be based on logic, or not. They may be based on fair, objective information, or biased and flawed perceptions. Nevertheless, they are starting to take an active role in their own social life. A role that requires respect and acknowledgment.

You and Kim presume that Sadie and Elizabeth will want to play together simply because they have spent time together previously and they will both be at the same place at the same time. This presumption is valid for preschool-aged children, but it may not be for first graders. Now, just because Sadie has an opinion about how she wants to spend her day does not imply that she has the power and authority to dictate her mother's social life. What it does require is the application of **shared control** between you and Sadie.

Shared control allows the adult to determine the overall goal for the next activity, but it allows the child some choice over a reasonable number of aspects. While it is unreasonable to surrender complete control over the afternoon's activities to a young child; it is also unreasonable to authoritatively assert complete control over every detail of the day. You provided an opportunity for shared control when you determined that Sadie and Elizabeth would be spending the afternoon together and Sadie and Elizabeth were expected to take turns choosing what game to play. Yet, you permitted Sadie to determine the reward (buy a new dress for her doll) for meeting your expectations. In another story, you permitted Sadie to choose to spend the day with her new friend, Becca, but you set the criteria for how she should behave (take turns, share, be kind, use manners). Finally, Sadie was permitted to choose the reward.

Shared control allows the parent to retain an appropriate amount of power in a relationship by setting expectations, but it allows the child to assert an appropriate amount of choice and freedom. This allows for some flexibility and autonomy. An easy way to remember this is to **provide choices within reason** (i.e., "Would you like broccoli or peas with your dinner?" Or, "Would you like to brush your teeth before, or after you take a bath?"). Shared control empowers the parent to maintain the appropriate level of authority to ensure that your expectations are communicated, but it provides your child an appropriate level of autonomy. In this way, your child is making a choice to cooperate, rather than being forced to comply.

There are so many aspects of a child's life over which they have little to no control (where they live and go to school, what teacher they have, what time they go to bed and wake up, etc.), it is reasonable to expect them to want to assert what little power and choice they do have when the opportunity presents itself. Yet, parents must ensure that they provide structure and guidance so that they can communicate their expectations and values and encourage responsible decision-making. Allowing young children to make small decisions when they are young provides practice and learning opportunities for when they need to make big decisions when they are older. You cannot choose your child's friends, but you can encourage them to make good choices.

Play Skills May Need To Be Taught

Play requires the coordination of social, communication, motor, emotional regulation and executive functioning skills. Many times, setting the expectation that two children can negotiate, collaborate, and cooperate while socializing together may be unreasonable. Children may lack the requisite skills to meet those expectations. Just as you would not take your child to the top of a mountain and communicate the expectation that they ski a "black diamond" expert run perfectly without receiving sufficient previous instruction, it is not reasonable to expect a child to navigate a complex social situation without sufficient experience and instruction. Thankfully, play skills are easily taught, and fun to learn.

When children develop play skills, they are placed in a position to not only succeed in life, but also enjoy doing so. Research* has shown the benefits of play to include the following:

- Play has immediate benefits, such as cardiovascular fitness, and long- term benefits, including a sense of morality and learning how to learn
- Play develops neural pathways in the brain
- Play enhances early development by at least 33%
- Toy play at age 18 months is related to the child's intelligence at age 3 years
- Play improves creativity, social skills, emotional regulation and executive functioning (i.e., impulse control, organization and planning).

When Sadie and Elizabeth struggled to play appropriately with one another, it may have been due to a combination of lack of supervision and a lack of play skills. Pillow fights are fun, throwing rocks is fun, getting attention is fun. Weren't Sadie and Elizabeth told to "have fun?" Why, from their perspective, should they be doing anything else? Certainly, communicating the expectation to have fun, but don't break anything, may have helped, but Sadie and Elizabeth required **"scaffolding"** of their play so that they could learn to **adapt** their play, **accommodate** each other's interests, and **be flexible**.

* Bodrova, Elena, and Deborah J. Leong. Tools of the Mind: *The Vygotskian Approach to Early Childhood Education*. 2nd ed. Upper Saddle River, N.J.: Pearson/Merrill Prentice Hall, 2007.

Diamond, Adele. "Want to Optimize Executive Functions and Academic Outcomes?: Simple, Just Nourish the Human Spirit." In *Minnesota Symposia on Child Psychology*, 37:205. NIH Public Access, 2014. http://www.ncbi.nlm.nih.gov/pmc/articles/PMC4210770/.

Robinson, Ken, and Lou Aronica. *Creative schools: the grassroots revolution that's transforming education*, 2015.

Stahmer, Aubyn. "It's fun to have fun, but you need to know how: Teaching object play using PRT." presented at the 3rd International Pivotal Response (PRT) Conference for ASD, Santa Barbara, CA, September 10, 2010.

Adults are challenged to demonstrate these social skills. Everyone requires some support to do so. When you are confronted with competing needs to support Kim, and also ensure that Sadie and Elizabeth play together appropriately, you say, "I really want to be here for you. But give me two seconds to get the girls on the same page. I know it'll buy us more time to talk." This allows you to set the girls up to play Twister (or, in another story, start an art project). Once the skill deficit of choosing an appropriate activity and initiating it calmly, flexibly, and cooperatively is **"scaffolded"** by you, you're able to devote your attention to Kim with the confidence of knowing that the girls possess sufficient skills to meet your clearly-defined expectations.

Multi-Tasking Rarely Works

How do you perform multiple roles successfully? Can you be a friend, a parent, a spouse and an employee, and succeed at all of these roles? It is very difficult, to be sure, but there are some ground rules that do help:

1. **Plan ahead:** How long could you envision your child behaving appropriately with little or no supervision while on a playdate? Divide that number in half and set a timer. Plan to interrupt yourself and stop what you are doing at this time so that you can monitor your child and praise him or her for good behavior. Would you rather have your conversation or work interrupted by your child's misbehavior, or interrupt the conversation on your terms, at a time you designate, when you could honestly predict a high likelihood that your child is still behaving well?

2. **Be honest** about your strengths, but also your weaknesses—it makes you authentic. Sometimes, all you can do is admit you love your child, but lack the skills to fix their problem immediately. You are not a seamstress, but you love your daughter very much, and will try hard to repair her bunny. You are not a marital therapist, but you do care about Kim's well-being, and can remember the times in their life when they were "in a better place," having fun and experiencing less stress. Showing support and empathy are powerful ways to "be there" for your friends and family, even if you lack the expertise to create an immediate solution to their problem.

3. **Be Present:** Put away your phone and make eye contact with your child, your friend, or whomever you are speaking to. So often, parents complain that their child cannot sustain their attention, but, in fact, it is adults who get distracted by all of the intrusions of modern life. When is the last time you provided 10 consecutive minutes of uninterrupted attention to your child? With no checking a text, your watch, or thinking about your to-do list, can you honestly report that you have been 100% present with him or her? Try it! You will be inclined to do it more and more, as you will begin to see the world through their eyes and re-experience the wonder of a few moments spent noticing how leaves blow in the wind, clouds form shapes in the sky, and your child's eyes sparkle when they look at you with innocence and love. When speaking with adults, you'll notice that your good mood will positively enhance theirs, and your interest in their life will pull you out of the stress of yours. Human connection happens when you are deliberately present in the moment. It takes practice but will become a great habit.

Bribery Is Not The Same As Positive Reinforcment

The key differences between the two are who is in control of the transaction, and when the incentive is offered. If, proactively, a parent determines that what they are expecting of their child is worthy of some form of reward, and the parent communicates this prior to placing the expectation in front of the child, it is positive reinforcement. In contrast, if the child determines that what they are being asked is something they are unwilling to do unless they are provided with a reward, then it is bribery. When Kim asks Elizabeth to clean her room, she didn't intend to offer her a cupcake. It was only after Elizabeth refused to clean her room that Kim resorted to the bribe of a cupcake. If this pattern plays out repeatedly (like when Elizabeth refuses to come upstairs unless she gets another cupcake), Elizabeth will learn to initially refuse to do everything she is asked to do. That way, she can receive treats for meeting the bare minimum of expectations.

In contrast, Kim should have a conversation with Elizabeth and say, "Elizabeth, it is going to take a lot of work to get the house clean prior to your playdate. If you clean your entire room, and you help with some additional cleaning, then I will be very proud of you. I might even give you a cupcake for dessert after lunch." Three ingredients are necessary for positive reinforcement to be effective:

1. The agreement regarding the expectations should clearly define the criterion for social praise (cleaning her room), and the criterion for exceeding the expectation and receiving a tangible reward, such as a cupcake (cleaning her room very well and helping with additional cleaning).

2. Tangible rewards should only be given in conjunction with social praise (i.e., I will be very proud of you and you will receive a cupcake).

3. The agreement must take place prior to defining the expectations, not after the child refuses to meet your expectations.

Because Kim had no intention of offering a cupcake to Elizabeth, offering one only after Elizabeth refused to cooperate placed all of the power in the hands of a child who is refusing to comply, rather than with the parent who is in charge of placing expectations on her child. Don't empower an uncooperative child by offering bribes. The last thing an uncooperative child needs is a stronger sense of entitlement. Bribery promotes and rewards uncooperative behavior.

Parents are in charge of setting expectations for their child. Providing incentives proactively encourages cooperation and may enhance motivation and effort. Attend to your child as they begin a task. When you "catch" your child making progress toward meeting your expectations, specifically label and praise their effort ("Thank you for cooperating and cleaning so well. Putting those shirts in the basket is a great start!"). Attending to, labeling, and praising your child should always be your primary method of reinforcement.

Explain the logical consequences of positive behavior. In the first story when you pull over to have a chat with Sadie, you say, "If you try to be patient, play her game nicely, and agree to the plan we come up with, that would make me so proud of you. And, do you know what I love to do when I am proud of you?"

"What?" Elizabeth asks.

"I like to do nice things for YOU! What is something nice I could do for you after you play nicely with Elizabeth?"

This conversation "connects the dots" for Sadie and clarifies the cause-effect relationship between her efforts to be flexible, take turns, and be patient and the positive outcome of making you proud. It also clarifies that when Sadie makes you proud, her life gets better because you do nice things for her. The occasional addition of tangible rewards (i.e., a new dress for her doll) is merely a "token" of your appreciation of her hard work and cooperation.

Tangible rewards are a "bonus" that strengthen the potency of positive reinforcement. The primary strength of parental influence is subtle and develops over time. As Elizabeth is more cooperative, Kim will become more inclined to say "yes" to her when she asks for things; when Elizabeth is less cooperative, Kim will be less inclined to say "yes" to her when she asks for things. As this pattern plays out, children typically start to ask questions, such as, "What can I do to earn a cupcake? Can I clean my room now? What if I also clean up the kitchen?" When that happens, you are no longer in a power struggle. You and your child are aligned with the mutual goals of her being cooperative and helpful, and her receiving tangible rewards and your social praise.

Do not underestimate how difficult it is to learn to "play nicely with others." Adults in the workplace often fail because they lack the social skills to work cooperatively with others. By attending to, supporting, and reinforcing these skills while your children are young, you are laying the foundation for their future success in life. Over time, your children will learn that good things happen to those who choose to cooperate and be helpful.

CPSIA information can be obtained
at www.ICGtesting.com
Printed in the USA
LVHW061243060319
609644LV00060B/484/P

9 781722 445904